Sara Swan Miller

Beetles

The Most Common Insects

Scholastic Inc.
New York • Toronto • London • Auckland • Sydney
Mexico City • New Delhi • Hong Kong
Danbury, Connecticut

For Jaik,

Didn't you always want to be a rock star like them?

Photographs ©: Animals Animals: 17 (John Pontier), 12, 13 (TC Nature); BBC Natural History Unit: 33 (Geoff Dore); Dembinsky Photo Assoc.: 5 bottom left (E. R. Degginger), 15 (Michael P. Gadomski), 29 (Gary Meszaros), 1 (Rod Planck); Frederick D. Atwood: 43; Peter Arnold Inc.: 5 top right (M. & C. Photography), 5 bottom right, 19 (John R. MacGregor), 5 top left, 42 (Hans Pfletschinger), 39 (Ed Reschke); Photo Researchers: 6 (Dr. John Brackenbury/SPL), 21 (Nigel Cattlin/Holt Studios), 41 (Ken Lax), 7 bottom (John Mitchell), cover (J. H. Robinson), 23 (L. West); Steve Marshall: 35; Visuals Unlimited: 7 top, 24, 25 (Bill Beatty), 31 (John D. Cunningham), 40 (Tom Edwards), 26, 27 (Jane McAlonan), 37 (Glenn Oliver).

Illustrations by Jose Gonzalez and Steve Savage

The photo on the cover shows a giant stag beetle and a ladybug. The photo on the title page shows a snout beetle.

Library of Congress Cataloging-in-Publication Data

Miller, Sara Swan
    Beetles: The most common insects / Sara Swan Miller
        p. cm. — (Animals in order)
    Includes bibliographical references and index.
    Summary: An introduction to beetles, the largest taxonomic order of insects, that includes descriptions of fourteen species and recommendations for finding, identifying, and observing them.
    ISBN 0-531-11629-8 (lib. bdg.)   0-531-13956-5 (pbk.)
1. Beetles—Juvenile literature. [1. Beetles.] I. Title. II. Series.
QL576. 2.M56   2001
595.76—dc21

Printed in Mexico
2 3 4 5 6 7 8 9 10 R 10 09 08 07 06

Contents

What Is a Beetle?

"What are those bugs doing on that plant?" "Why are all those flies buzzing around the porch light?" Have you ever asked questions like that? Chances are, you weren't looking at bugs or flies. Most likely, those "bugs" were beetles.

There are more beetles than any other kind of insect in the world. Scientists have identified more than 350,000 kinds of beetles, and there are many more left to discover. Some scientists think there may be as many as 8 million species of beetles! They live almost every-where on Earth—from the wettest, hottest jungles to the driest deserts. The only continent beetles don't live on is Antarctica.

Look at the four insects on the next page. Although one is called a "fly" and another is called a "bug," they are all beetles. Do you know what they have in common?

Lady beetle

Red milkweed beetle

Elephant stag beetle

Firefly

Traits of the Beetles

When you see a beetle, you might notice its front wings first. They are thick and hard. Those wings are called *elytra* (EL-ih-truh). When a beetle rests, its elytra lie flat and protect the fragile flight wings underneath.

When a beetle flies, it holds its elytra out straight and moves its second pair of wings. The elytra give the beetle added lift and help it balance. Beetles are slow, clumsy fliers. They look like tiny airborne trucks in low gear. But they get where they need to go.

Like other insects, beetles have a hard, tough outer skin called an *exoskeleton*. A beetle's exoskeleton is stronger than that of most insects. It protects the beetle and keeps its body from drying out in hot weather.

A soldier beetle in flight

6

All beetles have chewing mouthparts. Most beetles chew solid food, and a few also drink liquids, such as sap and nectar. Some beetles eat plants. Others eat wood, dead animals, animal droppings, or smaller insects.

A young beetle is called a *grub*. As it grows, the grub sheds its exoskeleton several times. Then it changes into a *pupa*. A beetle in the pupa stage looks like a pale beetle-mummy. Finally, the pupa changes into an adult.

The smallest and largest insects in the world are both beetles. The smallest beetle is about the same size as a period on this page. The largest beetle is bigger than your hand.

Beetles live in almost every kind of *habitat* on Earth—from woods to fields to deserts to ponds. Some beetles collect moisture under their wings. When they travel to a desert, they carry their own water with them. Others can stay underwater by breathing air they have trapped under their wings. Once you start looking, you'll find beetles everywhere!

A tiger beetle attacking a fly

A ladybug pupa

The Order of Living Things

A tiger has more in common with a house cat than with a daisy. A true bug is more like a butterfly than a jellyfish. Scientists arrange living things into groups based on how they look and how they act. A tiger and a house cat belong to the same group, but a daisy belongs to a different group.

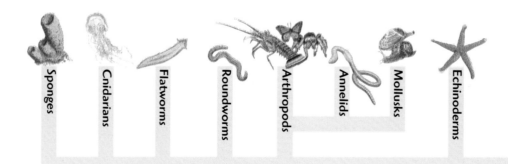

Sponges   Cnidarians   Flatworms   Roundworms   Arthropods   Annelids   Mollusks   Echinoderms

Animals

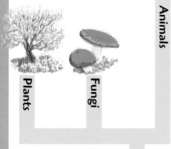

Plants   Fungi

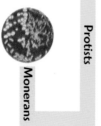

Monerans   Protists

All living things can be placed in one of five groups called *kingdoms*: the plant kingdom, the animal kingdom, the fungus kingdom, the moneran kingdom, or the protist kingdom. You can probably name many of the creatures in the plant and animal kingdoms. The fungus kingdom includes mushrooms, yeasts, and molds. The moneran and protist kingdoms contain thousands of living things that are too small to see without a microscope.

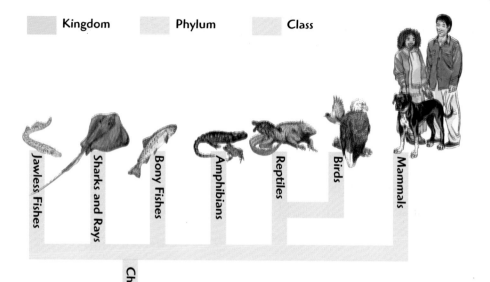

Kingdom   Phylum   Class

Jawless Fishes

Sharks and Rays

Bony Fishes

Amphibians

Reptiles

Birds

Mammals

Chordates

Because there are millions and millions of living things on Earth, some of the members of one kingdom may not seem all that similar. The animal kingdom includes creatures as different as tarantulas and trout, jellyfish and jaguars, salamanders and sparrows, elephants and earthworms.

To show that an elephant is more like a jaguar than an earthworm, scientists further separate the creatures in each kingdom into more specific groups. The animal kingdom can be divided into nine *phyla*. Humans belong to the chordate phylum. Almost all chordates have a backbone.

Each phylum can be subdivided into many *classes*. Humans, mice, and elephants all belong to the mammal class. Each class can be further divided into *orders*; orders into *families*, families into *genera*, and genera into *species*. All the members of a species are very similar.

How Beetles Fit In

You can probably guess that beetles belong to the animal kingdom. They have much more in common with spiders and snakes than with maple trees and morning glories.

Beetles belong to the arthropod phylum. All arthropods have an exoskeleton. Can you guess what other living things might be arthropods? Examples include spiders, scorpions, mites, ticks, millipedes, and centipedes. Some arthropods live in the ocean. Lobsters, crabs, and shrimps all belong to this group.

The arthropod phylum can be divided into a number of classes. Beetles belong to the insect class. Butterflies, ants, flies, and true bugs are also insects.

There are thirty different orders of insects. The beetles make up one of these orders. The scientific name of this order is *coleoptera* (koh-lee-AHP-tuh-ruh), which means "sheath-wing." As you learned earlier, beetles have a set of hard outer wings that protect their underwings.

The beetles can be divided into a number of different families and genera. These groups can be broken down into thousands of species. Are you ready to find out more about fourteen interesting kinds of beetles?

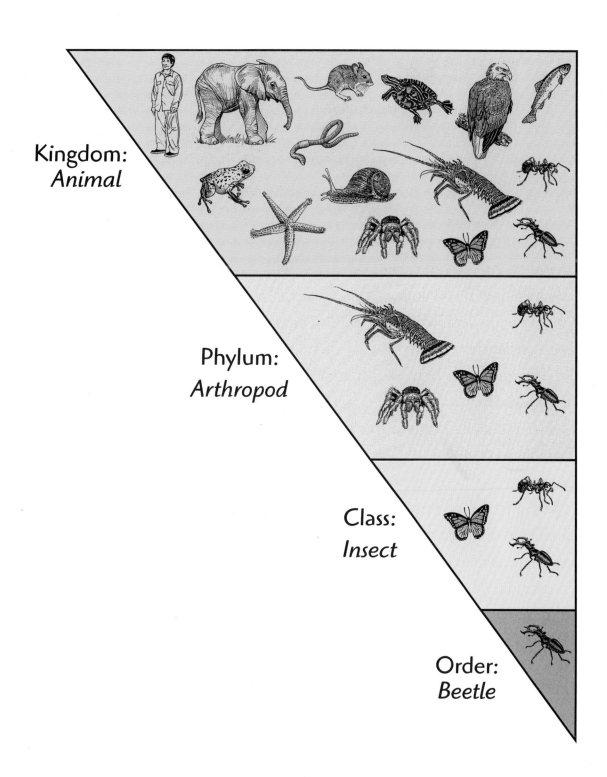

Kingdom:
Animal

Phylum:
Arthropod

Class:
Insect

Order:
Beetle

Stag Beetles
FAMILY: Lucanidae
COMMON EXAMPLE: Giant stag beetle
GENUS AND SPECIES: *Lucanus elaphus*
SIZE: 1 to 2 inches (2.5 to 5 cm)

If you ever see a male stag beetle, you will understand how this insect got its name. Its huge jaws, called *mandibles*, look like the antlers of a stag, or male deer. Male stag beetles use their mandibles the way stags use their antlers—to fight with each other during mating season.

The giant stag beetle's mandibles are truly enormous. They look as though they could give you a horrible bite. You might be surprised to learn that the bigger a stag beetle's jaws are, the weaker they are. Female stag beetles have smaller mandibles, so they can bite much harder.

Despite their fierce look, giant stag beetles are harmless. The adults lap up plant juices and sap. Sometimes they feed on the *honey-dew* that comes out of the tails of tiny insects called *aphids*. The grubs live inside old logs or tree stumps and feed on decaying wood. They may take as long as 6 years to become adults.

Click Beetles

FAMILY: Elateridae
COMMON EXAMPLE: Eastern eyed click beetle
GENUS AND SPECIES: *Alaus oculatus*
SIZE: 1 to 1 3/4 inches (2.5 to 4.5 cm)

When most insects land on their back, they have a hard time getting right side up. But a click beetle has a good trick for solving that problem. It arches its back, then slaps it down again. With a loud click, it flips end over end. The beetle may fly 6 inches (15 cm) into the air! Sometimes it lands on its feet and goes scurrying away. At other times, the beetle lands on its back again. It keeps trying, though, clicking and flipping until it finally lands right side up.

Unlike other insects, the click beetle's *thorax*—the part of the body its legs grow from—is hinged. A long spine on one part of the thorax fits into a groove in the other part. The click you hear when the beetle slaps its back on the ground is the sound of the spine clicking into that groove.

A click beetle's clicking and flipping can startle enemies too. The eastern eyed click beetle has another way of protecting itself. The spots on its back look like big eyes. When a bird sees the click beetle, the bird thinks those "eyes" belong to a much bigger animal. The bird doesn't want to tackle anything *that* big!

14

Eastern eyed click beetle grubs are called wireworms. Farmers hate them because they live underground for years, feeding on corn, potatoes, wheat, and other crops.

Scarab Beetles

FAMILY: Scarabaeidae
COMMON EXAMPLE: Tumblebug
GENUS AND SPECIES: *Dichotomius carolinus*
SIZE: 1/2 inch (1 cm)

If you happen to be out in a field some evening, you might be lucky enough to see a pair of tumblebugs behaving in a very odd way. These small beetles scurry along backward, pushing a ball of *dung*, or animal droppings, over the ground. Eventually, they stop and dig a tunnel. Then they push the ball inside. The female lays an egg in the ball and covers it up with dirt. When the grub hatches, it will have plenty of dung to eat.

Tumblebugs are helpful creatures. They not only keep a pasture clean, but also help fertilize it. Tumblebug grubs share the dung with *bacteria*, which break down buried dung into fertile soil that growing plants need.

Sometimes adult tumblebugs dig themselves into the ground along with a ball of animal droppings. There they stay, safe and sound, eating away until the dung is all gone. Then off they go to find more. In 24 hours, a tumblebug can eat more than its own weight in dung!

Fireflies

FAMILY: Lampyridae
COMMON EXAMPLE: Pyralis firefly
GENUS AND SPECIES: *Photinus pyralis*
SIZE: 1/2 inch (1 cm)

What is sweeter than a warm summer evening filled with the soft flashes of silent fireflies? Children all over the world love running through fields, trying to catch these fascinating insects.

Fireflies light up to attract mates. As a male flies along, he flashes his light in a special pattern. A female, waiting on a plant, flashes the same signal back so that the male can find her. Each species has its own pattern so that fireflies can find the right mates.

The females of one species do a tricky thing. They copy the light pattern that another species of firefly makes. When a male flies down to mate, the copycat female gobbles him up! Most other adult fireflies feed on pollen or nectar. Some don't eat at all. Firefly grubs live on the ground and eat other insects, slugs, and snails.

How does a firefly make its light? It stores special chemicals inside its tail. When the firefly takes in air through a breathing tube on its tail, oxygen mixes with the chemicals and makes light.

19

Lady Beetles

FAMILY: Coccinellidae
COMMON EXAMPLE: Two-spotted lady beetle
GENUS AND SPECIES: *Adalia bipunctata*
SIZE: 1/2 inch (1 cm)

The two-spotted lady beetle gets its name from the number of black spots on its shiny orange back. Other species of lady beetles can have seven, nine, thirteen, or fifteen spots. Some species have no spots at all. Lady beetles, which are also called ladybugs, are definitely a farmer's friends. They eat aphids and other creatures that destroy crops. On average, a lady beetle will eat 5,000 aphids during its lifetime.

Sometimes farmers and gardeners have so many aphids in their fields that they buy large bags of ladybugs and set them free among the crops. Many times, ants guard the aphids, though. Ants like to lap up the sweet honeydew the aphids make.

When lady beetles come across ants guarding aphids, a battle breaks out. The ants bite fiercely at the lady beetles, and the beetles fight back. If there are enough lady beetles, they chase the ants away. After the ants retreat, the lady beetles gobble up all the aphids.

Many species of lady beetles *hibernate* in large groups under stones or loose bark. They often return to the same place year after year. That makes it easy for people to collect the beetles and sell them to farmers.

A single female lady beetle can lay as many as 1,000 eggs at a time, and she may lay eggs several times a year. A grub often eats about 400 aphids as it grows into a pupa.

Checkered Beetles

FAMILY: Cleridae
COMMON EXAMPLE: Red-blue checkered
  beetle
GENUS AND SPECIES: *Trichodes nutalli*
SIZE: 3/8 inch (1 cm)

Like the two-spotted lady beetle, the red-blue checkered beetle is a pretty insect. If you ever notice one resting on a daisy in a flower-filled meadow, watch it closely. It might munch on some pollen or pounce on a small insect that passes by. The red-blue checkered beetle is one of the few beetles that eats other insects.

In the spring, the female red-blue checkered beetle lays her eggs on flowers. When a grub hatches, it waits patiently for a bee to come looking for nectar. Then it hitches a ride on the bee's back. The bee carries the grub back to its nest, unaware that it's bringing home an enemy. The grub gets right to work eating up the bee larvae.

There are about 3,000 species of checkered beetles. Most of them are brightly colored. They come in many checkered color combinations—red, yellow, orange, green, and black.

Many checkered beetles feed on insects that dig into trees and kill them. Others gobble up caterpillars that destroy crops. Some lay their eggs on the egg pods of grasshoppers. When the grubs hatch, they eat the grasshopper eggs.

Blister Beetles

FAMILY: Meloidae
COMMON EXAMPLE: Short-winged blister beetle
GENUS AND SPECIES: *Meloe augusticollis*
SIZE: 1/2 inch (1 cm)

Can you guess how the blister beetle got its name? If you pick one up, you'll soon find out! The blister beetle is also called the oil beetle. It is covered with an oily liquid that burns the skin and causes big, watery blisters to form.

Many blister beetles are brightly colored or jet black. They don't need to hide from enemies. Birds and other *predators* usually leave them alone. Unlike other beetles, blister beetles can't fly. Their elytra are very short, and they do not have a second pair of wings. They spend their days crawling over the plants they feed on.

The life cycle of a short-winged blister beetle is more complicated than that of other beetles. A female lays as many as 10,000 eggs on the ground. Each tiny, bristly grub climbs up a plant stem and waits for a hairy insect to come by. If a female bee passes, the grub grabs on to her and holds on tight

24

while the bee makes her nest. While the bee is laying her eggs, the grub slips off the bee and clings to one of the eggs. The outer covering of the egg hardens around the grub. It is safe inside the egg—and has plenty of food.

As the grub grows, its legs become shorter and shorter. Eventually, it can't move at all. It spends the winter that way, then turns into an active grub again. Finally, it becomes a pupa and then, at last, an adult.

Long-Horned Beetles

FAMILY: Cerambycidae
COMMON EXAMPLE: Red milkweed beetle
GENUS AND SPECIES: *Tetraopes tetraophthalmus*
SIZE: 1/2 inch (1 cm)

It's easy to spot a red milkweed beetle on a milkweed plant. The insect's red and black colors really stand out. Like many other brightly colored insects, the milkweed beetle is giving birds a warning: "Don't eat me! I taste bad!"

Milkweed beetles feed on the juice of milkweed plants. They don't mind the bad taste. Have you ever heard the expression, "You are what you eat"? Milkweed beetles taste as bad to predators as the juice they feed on!

A red milkweed beetle has another way of protecting itself. If a bird picks it up, the beetle squeaks! It makes this sound by rubbing two parts of its body together. The squeaking usually startles the bird so much that it drops the beetle. If you pick up a red milkweed beetle, it will do the same thing. Be careful, though! This beetle could give you a nip.

Females lay their eggs on milkweed stems near the ground. The grubs bore into the plant's roots and spend the winter there. In the spring, they become pupae and then adults. Then they make their way up the stem to the topmost flowers.

26

A red milkweed beetle's scientific name means "four-eyed." If you look closely at its eyes with a hand lens, you'll see that each of its two *compound eyes* is divided into two parts. Many insects have eyes made up of separate visual units, but this beetle really looks as though it has four eyes.

Whirligig Beetles

FAMILY: *Gyrinidae*
COMMON EXAMPLE: Large whirligig beetle
GENUS AND SPECIES: *Dineutus americanus*
SIZE: 1/2 inch (1 cm)

Have you ever seen a cluster of whirligig beetles spinning in circles on the surface of a pond? No matter how quickly they zip about, they never bump into one another. How do they do that?

A whirligig beetle's short antennae sense movement on the surface of the water. They help the beetle avoid bumping into its companions. They also tell the beetle when another insect falls into the water. As the insect struggles wildly, the whirligig beetle zips over and gobbles it up.

A whirligig beetle's eyes are divided into two parts, so the beetle can see above and below the water's surface at the same time. This means the beetle can search for *prey* underwater and still be on the lookout for enemies above the water.

A whirligig grub looks like a tiny centipede. It lives underwater and hunts for the larvae of other insects. When it captures prey, it uses the four long, sharp hooks on its tail to hold on to a stick or plant. When the grub is ready to become a pupa, it crawls ashore and hangs upside down from a stem or branch. Then it scoops up a few mouthfuls of dirt and mixes it with saliva to make a pupal case. The pupa lives in the case until it becomes an adult.

Water Scavenger Beetles

FAMILY: Hydrophilidae
COMMON EXAMPLE: Giant water scavenger
  beetle
GENUS AND SPECIES: *Hydrophilus triangularis*
SIZE: 1 to 1 1/2 inches (2.5 to 4 cm)

Water scavenger beetles prowl about in stagnant water near the edges of ponds. They are searching for decaying plants and animals they like to eat. By eating rotting materials, the beetles also help keep ponds clean. Sometimes water scavenger beetles also eat live insects.

When these beetles swim, they kick their flat, paddle-shaped back legs alternately, like a swimmer doing the crawl. Every now and then, the beetles rise to the surface of the water. They pump air around their bodies, coating their undersides with a silvery envelope. Then they dive down again, taking along their own air supply as a human diver does.

The grubs have huge heads and very long mandibles. They are fierce hunters. They swim about underwater, gobbling up other insects. Sometimes they even eat one another!

Some adult water scavenger beetles work busily all year long—even when ice covers their pond. In the summer, they sometimes fly off to other places. Look for them fluttering around your porch light on a summer evening.

Predaceous Diving Beetles

FAMILY: Dytiscidae
COMMON EXAMPLE: Great diving beetle
GENUS AND SPECIES: *Dytiscus marginalis*
SIZE: 1 to 1 1/2 inches (2.5 to 4 cm)

The great diving beetle is the champion hunter of the pond. It will eat anything it can grab. With its strong jaws, this beetle can gobble up animals much larger than itself. Sometimes it eats tadpoles or fish twice its size!

Diving beetles are well suited to life underwater. Their smooth, streamlined bodies glide quickly through the pond. Their flattened back legs work like oars. Most other water beetles move their legs alternately, but the large diving beetle moves its legs at the same time. Fringes on the edges of its legs help the beetle swim even faster.

A diving beetle can stay underwater for a long time. When it needs more air, it sticks the breathing tube on its tail up above the surface. The tube collects a bubble of air under the beetle's elytra. The insect uses that air to breathe during its next dive.

Diving beetle grubs are just as fierce as the adults. They wiggle about hunting for other insects, snails, and small fish. They grab prey with their long, sickle-shaped mandibles. Then they pump digestive juices into the prey to turn its insides to slush. The grubs slurp up the slush and discard the animal's hard shell.

In Asia, people raise diving beetles for food. Children there think of them as a special treat! How would you like to munch on a crunchy diving beetle?

Ground Beetles

FAMILY: Carabidae
COMMON EXAMPLE: Bombardier beetle
GENUS AND SPECIES: *Brachinus crepitans*
SIZE: 1/4 to 1/2 inch (0.5 to 1 cm)

As evening falls, a bombardier beetle creeps along the muddy ground. It is hunting for insects to eat. Suddenly, a hungry toad plops down next to the beetle. The bombardier beetle has a surprise for the toad, though. Pop! Pop! Pop! The beetle fires puffs of boiling hot, stinging gas right in the toad's face! The gas stings the startled toad's eyes, giving the beetle a chance to scurry away.

The bombardier beetle stores two different chemicals in chambers near its tail. When the beetle is startled, it releases both chemicals into a third chamber. When these chemicals mix, they explode out of the beetle's tail. A bombardier beetle can reload and fire up to a dozen times if necessary.

The females lay their eggs in blobs of mud on stones or plants. When a grub hatches, it looks for a water beetle pupa hiding in its chamber underground. After it eats the pupa, the grub spends the winter in the chamber. In spring, the bombardier beetle comes out fully grown, ready to raise its tail and defend itself.

Carrion Beetles

FAMILY: Silphidae
COMMON EXAMPLE: Margined burying
   beetle
GENUS AND SPECIES: *Nicrophorus marginatus*
SIZE: 3/4 to 1 1/4 inches (2 to 3 cm)

Have you ever wondered why you rarely see dead animals, or *carrion*, lying around in the woods? You can thank the margined burying beetle and other kinds of carrion beetles.

Carrion beetles can smell a dead mouse up to 2 miles (3 km) away. When they pick up a scent, they rush to the carcass and bury the dead animal. If the soil is loose, a pair of carrion beetles can bury a mouse in just a few minutes!

Why do carrion beetles bury dead animals? After they bury an animal, margined burying beetles remove its fur or feathers and work its flesh into a ball. Then they feed on the carrion ball. The females also lay their eggs on the ball. When the grubs hatch, they're surrounded by plenty of food.

Adult beetles take care of the grubs as they grow. The adults call to the grubs with a rasping sound that tells the young where to find food. When those grubs develop into pupae, the females lay more eggs.

The margined burying beetle is shiny black with bright orange markings. Those bright colors send a message: "Leave me alone! I

taste rotten!" Why do you think carrion beetles taste bad? As you
might guess, these beetles smell and taste like the rotting flesh they
live and feed on!

Tiger Beetles

FAMILY: Carabidae
COMMON EXAMPLE: Big sand tiger beetle
GENUS AND SPECIES: *Cicindela formosa*
SIZE: 1/2 inch (1 cm)

Can you guess how the tiger beetles got their name? Both the adults and the grubs are fierce predators. They also have distinctive white markings, similar to a tiger's. A big sand tiger beetle can kill and eat insects much larger than itself.

The long-legged adults can run up to 1 1/2 miles (2.4 km) an hour over the sand. When a big sand tiger beetle catches up with its prey, it grabs the insect with its strong, sickle-shaped jaws. Then it covers the prey with juices that start digesting the animal. Finally, the beetle chews and sucks on the prey until it is all gone.

The female digs a hole in the sand and lays a single egg. When the grub hatches, it digs a tunnel. The grub loosens the soil with its jaws and uses its head as a shovel. The grub may dig a hole more than 6 feet (2 m) deep! If the area around the hole floods, the grub can survive for up to 3 weeks by breathing air trapped in the tunnel.

Most of the time, the grub hides just inside the entrance of its tunnel, waiting for another insect to come along. The grub grabs the prey in its strong jaws and hangs on to the tunnel walls with special hooks on its body. Even a big, struggling insect can't free itself from the grub's grip. When the prey is dead, the grub eats it.

Looking for Beetles in Fields, Gardens, and Woods

Would you like to become a beetle expert? You don't need a lot of fancy equipment. Because there are so many species of beetles, you can find them almost anywhere.

You can look for beetles in a field or woodland, but you can also find them in a garden, in your backyard, or in a schoolyard. If you live in a city, you can find plenty of beetles at your local park.

The best way to find beetles in a field is to get down on your hands and knees with a hand lens. Gently part the grasses and other plants to find beetles close to the ground. Look closely at the leaves and stems.

Useful Tools

A sweep net

Small, clear plastic jars with lids

A plastic hand lens

A journal for recording what you find

A field guide to insects

In tall grass, a sweep net makes it easier to find beetles. Swish the net back and forth as you walk. Then look inside the net to see what you collected. Gently put the insects into a jar so that you can examine them more closely. When you have figured out which insects are beetles, keep them and let the rest go. Don't keep the beetles in the jar too long either. They may starve or suffocate.

In the woods, look carefully under the bark of trees and on the undersides of leaves. Look closely at plants growing near the ground too. Gently move rocks and sticks to see if beetles or grubs are hiding underneath.

When you find an insect, watch it for a while. Is it a beetle? Where is it going? What is it eating? After you figure out what the beetle is doing in its natural setting, carefully place it in a jar and look at it more closely with a hand lens. You can use your field guide to find out what kind of beetle you have found.

Draw a picture of each beetle in your journal. Describe how it moves, what

This boy is collecting beetles.

it eats, when and where you found it, and any other information you think is interesting. When you have done all of that, put the beetles back where you found them.

Looking for Beetles in Ponds and Streams

You may be surprised at how many beetles you can find in ponds and streams. All of them have found ways to solve special problems. How do they breathe underwater? How do they find food? Over millions of years, each kind of water beetle has found its own ways to adapt.

You can find beetles in every part of a pond—from the surface to the muddy bottom. Beetles live in streams too, especially in quiet pools with little or no moving current.

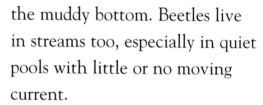

Useful Tools

A strainer, about 9 inches (23 cm) across

Two plastic dishpans

A tablespoon

A plastic hand lens

Small, clear plastic jars with lids

A journal for recording what you find

A field guide to pond and stream life

Before you collect any beetles, fill one dishpan half full with clear pond water. Use your strainer to scoop up some watery mud from the bottom of the pond. Put the mud in the other dishpan. Use the tablespoon to carefully search through the mud in the second dishpan. When you find an insect or an insect larva, use the spoon to put it in the dishpan of clear water.

Now you can watch the insect easily. Is it a beetle or some other kind of insect? Notice how it moves. Float a leaf on the surface and see if the insect wants to hide in the shadow.

If you want to get a closer look, put the insect into a jar with some pond water and look at it with a hand lens. Look at its wings, mouthparts, and eyes. Can you figure out how it breathes?

When you have placed a few insects in the dishpan of clear water, watch closely. Do some of them eat others? You can find out more about them from your field guide. You can also use your strainer to scoop beetles from the surface of the water. Put them in the dishpan of clear water and watch what they do.

In your journal, write down everything you see. Draw pictures of the beetles you collect and record when and where you found each one.

When you have finished observing the beetles, lower each dishpan until it is just above the surface of the pond and gently pour the beetles back into the water.

Words to Know

aphid—a small insect that feeds on many kinds of plants

bacteria—a living thing in the moneran kingdom

carrion—the rotting flesh of dead animals

class—a group of creatures within a phylum that share certain characteristics

compound eyes—eyes that have separate visual units, such as many insects' eyes

dung—animal droppings

elytra—the hard outer wings of a beetle

exoskeleton—the tough, skinlike covering of insects and some other animals

family—a group of creatures within an order that share certain characteristics

genus (plural genera)—a group of creatures within a family that share certain characteristics

grub—the larva, or first life stage, of a beetle

habitat—the environment where a plant or animal lives and grows

hibernate—to rest or sleep for the winter

honeydew—a sweet juice that aphids make

kingdom—one of the five divisions into which all living things are placed: the animal kingdom, the plant kingdom, the fungus kingdom, the moneran kingdom, and the protist kingdom

mandible—a beetle's jaw

order—a group of creatures within a class that share certain characteristics

phylum (plural **phyla**)—a group of creatures within a kingdom that share certain characteristics

predator—an animal that eats other animals

prey—an animal that is hunted and eaten by another animal

pupa (plural **pupae**)—the second life stage of a beetle and many other insects

species—a group of creatures within a genus that share certain characteristics. Members of a species can mate and produce young.

thorax—the segment of an insect's body from which its legs grow

Learning More

Books

Evans, Arthur V., Charles L. Bellamy, and Lisa Charles Watson. *An Inordinate Fondness for Beetles*. New York: Henry Holt, 1996.

Ross, Michael Elsohn. *Ladybugology*. Minneapolis, MN: Carolrhoda Books, 1997.

Stewart, Melissa. *Insects*. Danbury, CT: Children's Press, 2001.

White, Richard E. *Beetles: A Field Guide to the Beetles of North America*. Boston: Houghton Mifflin Co., 1998.

CD-ROM

Bug Adventure: An Insect Adventure. Knowledge Adventure, 1995.

Web Sites

An Inordinate Fondness for Beetles
http://www.fond4beetles.com
This is an online version of the book by the same name (see above). Both include interesting, hard-to-find information and pictures.

Beetles
http://www.source.at/english/navigation.htm
This site includes photographs, games, sound, movies, and lots and lots of links to other sites.

Insecta Inspecta World
http://www.insecta-inspecta.com/beetles/scarab/index.html
This site has all kinds of information about insects, including beetles.

Index

About the Author

Sara Swan Miller has enjoyed working with children all her life, first as a Montessori nursery-school teacher and later as an outdoor environmental educator at the Mohonk Preserve in New Paltz, New York. As director of the preserve school program, Miller has led hundreds of schoolchildren on field trips and taught them the importance of appreciating and respecting the natural world, including its less lovable "creepy-crawlies."

Miller has written a number of children's books, including *Three Stories You Can Read to Your Dog*; *Three Stories You Can Read to Your Cat*; *Three More Stories You Can Read to Your Dog*; *What's in the Woods?: An Outdoor Activity Book*; *Oh, Cats of Camp Rabbitbone*; *Piggy in the Parlor and Other Tales*; *Better Than TV*; and *Will You Sting Me? Will You Bite?: The Truth About Some Scary-Looking Insects*. She has also written several books on farm animals for the Children's Press True Books series and several other books in the Animals in Order series.